Marnie & Rob
and the Christmas Parcel

Elisia Ray, Author
Aaron R, Illustrator
Tom McBrien, Editor

Marnie & Rob and the Christmas Parcel

ISBN: 978-1-0686428-2-1
Published by: Hiddenite Star Publisher
First Edition 2024

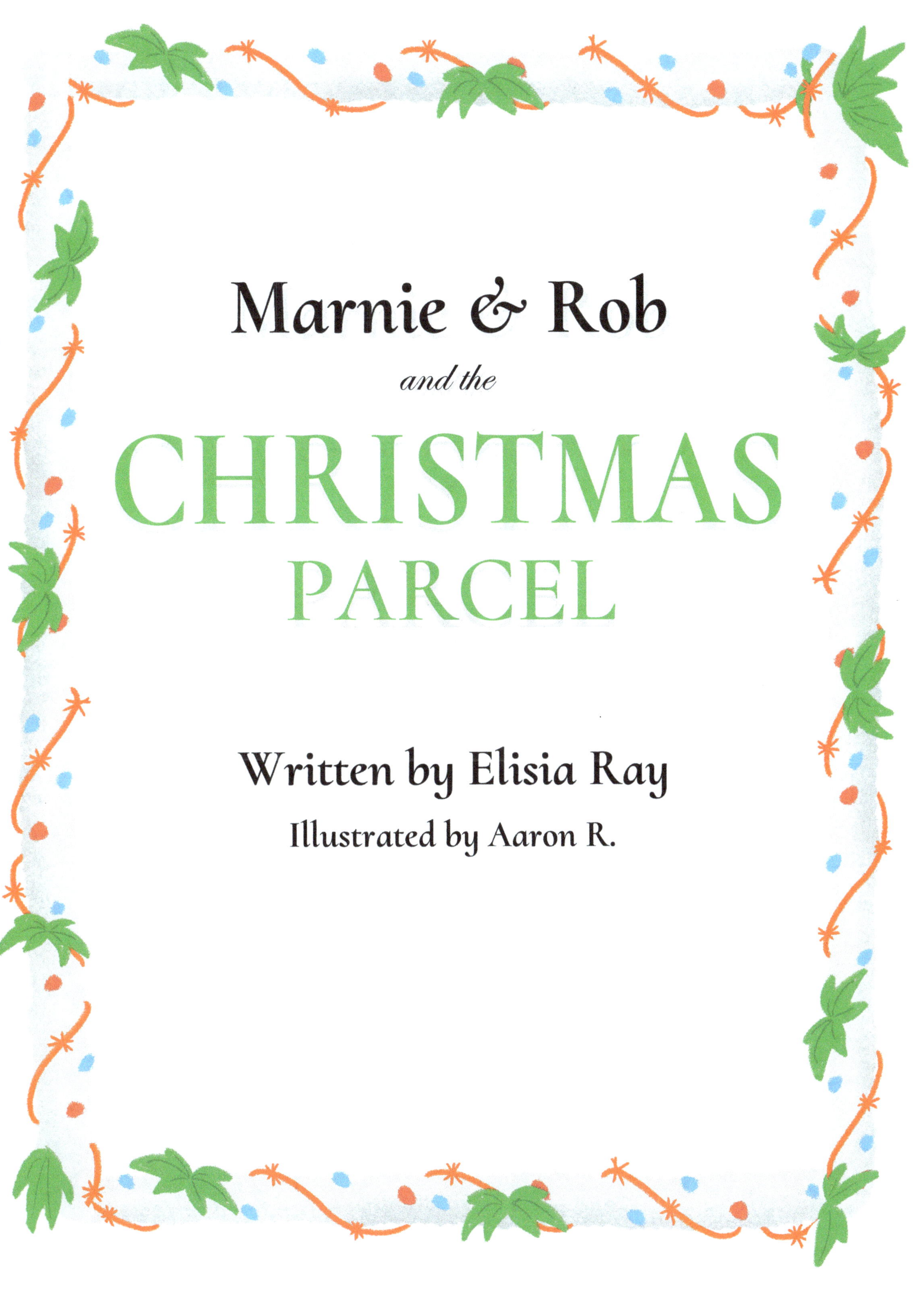

Marnie & Rob

and the

CHRISTMAS
PARCEL

Written by Elisia Ray

Illustrated by Aaron R.

For my Gran, Grandad and Maureen and Adrian

xx

KNOCK KNOCK!
"Who is that?" said Marnie, walking towards the door.

"Not sure!!' replied Rob.

"Good morning," said the Newfoundland post dog.
"I have a BIG delivery for Marnie and Rob!"

It was a huge green parcel with a red bow on top.

The parcel was pulled into the house.
"This is heavy," puffed Marnie.
"It sure is," said Rob,
perched on top of the parcel not helping at all.

They quickly unwrapped it.
    Inside was a big machine and a green envelope.

Marnie started to open the envelope and pulled the note out.

Rob took the note from Marnie and put it in his beak.
    "I'll read the note," said Rob excitedly.

"Dear Marnie and Rob,

Your ice cream was so yummy at our wedding,

so here is a new EMI.2416.

EMI means Electronic Machine Intelligence.

It will drive, make Christmas treats and make

fart noises! Merry Christmas!

Thanks again.

Enjoy

Bride & Groom

'Wow, this is amazing! I love it," said Rob happily.
"What do you think, Marnie?"

Marnie gave the new machine a suspicious
side-eye, and said, "There's nothing wrong
with the old cart."

Marnie looked around at
the rickety wooden blue cart,
which had all the yummy
ice cream inside.

Rob's eyes lit up. He had an idea.
"Maybe I could take the new EMI.2416 outside,
make some money and buy Marnie a secret Christmas present!"

Meanwhile, Marnie walked up to the glass jar in the kitchen. It was empty!
"I wanted to buy Rob a secret present," said Marnie sadly.

"I know, I'll take the ice cream cart out sell, some ice cream and buy a secret Christmas present for Rob," Marnie said to herself, wagging her tail.

Marnie walked back into the decorated front room.
Rob had gotten the machine up and running.
The EMI.2416 was ready to go!

"Right, I'm off to take the machine out for a spin.
I won't be long," said Rob.

"Ok," said Marnie,
    waving goodbye to Rob at the door.

Marnie headed back into the house.

RING RING!

It was the phone.
Marnie answered.
It was Grandma Hammond!

"Hello, am I still ok to come over for Christmas dinner and exchange Christmas presents later?"

"Yes, of course, Grandma.
I just need to nip outside for a little bit.
There's something I have to do first.
But I won't be long."

M&R
ICE CREAM

Marnie hangs up the phone and pulls the blue ice cream cart behind her.
She feels the chill of the cold winter air as she opens the door
and heads outside into the snowy outdoors.

Rob decided to bring the EMI.2416 to
the Cat Christmas market.

"I should be able to sell loads of Christmas treats here,"
he thought, flapping his wings happily.

He came across two Siamese cats.

"Do you have some candy cane nibbles, please?"
the cats asked at the same time.

Rob smiled. "Why, yes I do."

Luckily, the tortoiseshell cat was the last customer
when the EMI2416 said,
"Please charge me to continue,"
farted and then powered down.

"Oh no," said Rob. "I will have to leave it here.
At least I have enough money now to get Marnie a present."
He rushed to the shops before they shut.

Rob reached the shops in time,
 flew in and saw what he wanted straight away.
    "This please!"
     A few moments later, Rob came out with a paper bag.

"Time to get home. It's getting late.
  Marnie will wonder where I am, and this snow is getting really heavy now,"
    he thought to himself. Then off he went.

Back at the house.

Marnie was already back home. She had sold all her
ice creams and got her present for Rob.

"I wonder where Rob is," she thought.
She quickly put something under the tree and started on dinner.

Rob flew through the door.
Marnie wagged her tail,
"There you are!" she cried happily.
"Where's the EMI.2416?"

"Well..." began Rob.

KNOCK KNOCK!

"I'll get it, said Marnie.
Rob breathed a sigh of relief at not having to explain
what happened to the EMI.2416,
and quickly put something under the tree.

At the door, everyone was there! Gracie, Marnie's uncle, Uncle Jay, Grandma Hammond, Rob's cousins Shaney, Gordon, Adrian and Reeny, and their old friend, the Chinese crested dog.

"Come in, everyone," said Marnie.
"The Christmas dinner is nearly ready!"

"Smells delicious!" said Grandma Hammond.

Everyone sat around the table and enjoyed the food and drinks
and, of course, ice cream!
"Merry Christmas, everyone!" said Marnie and Rob happily together.

After everyone had gone and everything was tidied up, the pair noticed
there were still two more presents under the Christmas tree.
"Is that for me?" the pair said at the same time.

Marnie gave
the present a sniff

and Rob poked it
with his beak.

Then, they both spun around to
quickly unwrap it as fast as they could.

They both spun back around to each other to say thank you and realised
they were holding the same gift. A colourful Christmas jumper!

"Let's put them on," said Rob.
"Great idea," nodded Marnie.

"It's awesome! Merry Christmas," said Rob.

"It's the best present ever.
Merry Christmas," said Marnie.

Elisia is a Yorkshire lass with Carribean roots, her encounter with the real-life Marnie she shares with her partner inspired her to write children's books. She was once scared of dogs as a young child but now has grown to adore them.

Elisia has Multiple Sclerosis. Some days are tough she but has a zest for life and appreciates the little things the world has to offer.

Webpage www.elisiaray.com

ELISIA_WRITES